My Minotaur

Selected Poems 1998-2006
Keith Holyoak

Illustrations by
Jim Holyoak

DOS MADRES

2010

DOS MADRES PRESS INC.
P.O.Box 294, Loveland, Ohio 45140
www.dosmadres.com   editor@dosmadres.com

Dos Madres is dedicated to the belief that the small press is essential
to the vitality of contemporary literature as a carrier of the new voice,
as well as the older, sometimes forgotten voices of the past. And in an
ever more virtual world, to the creation of fine books pleasing to the
eye and hand.

Dos Madres is named in honor of Vera Murphy and Libbie Hughes,
the "Dos Madres" whose contributions have made this press possible.

Dos Madres Press, Inc, is an Ohio Not For Profit Corporation and a
501 (c) (3) qualified public charity. Contributions are tax deductible.

Executive Editor: Robert J. Murphy

Book Designer: Elizabeth H. Murphy
www.illusionstudios.net

Typset in Adobe Garamond Pro
& Treasure Map Deadhand

Library of Congress Control Number: 2009939321

First Edition

for our parents / grandparents

Violet Mary Holyoak (née Paton)
& James King Holyoak

"Mom, am I better than Wordsworth yet?"
The boy read his little song.
"Certainly coming along, my dear—
My yes, you're coming along!"

CONTENTS

Acknowledgements

I owe a debt of gratitude to the editors of periodicals where many of these poems first appeared (often as earlier versions): *Bellowing Ark, Candelabrum Poetry Magazine, Clark Street Review, Citizen 32, Edge City Review, Envoi, Flaming Arrows, Neovictorian/Cochlea, Orbis, Penwood Review, Poem, Poetry Salzburg Review, Raintown Review, Real Change, Red Rock Review, Romantics Quarterly, The Eclectic Muse, The London Magazine, The Lyric, Torre de Papel,* and *Tucumcari Literary Review.* Neil Harding McAlister included "The Happy Trout" in his anthology *New Classic Poems: Contemporary Verse that Rhymes* (2005), and "The Private Loves of Mr. and Mrs. Chen" in his *Rhyme and Reason: Modern Formal Poetry* (2006). I also thank the editors of websites that have posted some of my poems: The HyperTexts (www.thehypertexts.com), Black Cat Poems (www.blackcatpoems.com), and The Formalist Portal (www.theformalist.org). Airom Bleicher of Broken Electric Records produced a CD based on my poem "Descent".

Robert and Elizabeth Murphy of Dos Madres Press shared in the labors of creating this book. Many others contributed to the project in important if sometimes mysterious ways. I especially thank my friend Miriam Bassok, for serving so often as a gentle first reader, and my wife Hongjing Lu, for everything.

myself and other strangers

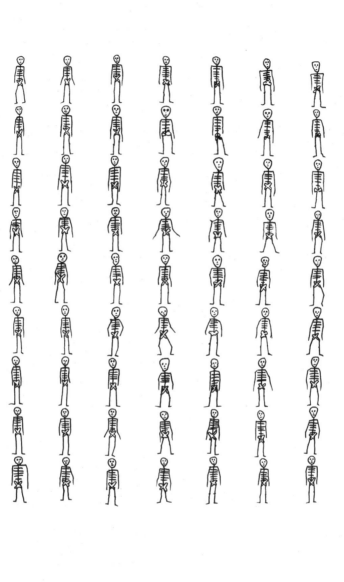

FIRE DRILL

The bell rang, but not the usual
Bell apportioning the school day—
This bell rang louder, harsher, with a cruel
Edge to it. Down plunged the breakaway
Shards of daydreams; pencils dropped,
Books slammed shut, and the students all
Looked up as the droning lesson stopped.
    The alarm stopped too, and a magical
Hush for a moment held the classroom still—
A disembodied voice called out, "Fire drill!"

    "Fire drill!" the children echoed back,
And rose in glee, for the bland routine
Of a slow school day, thrown off track,
Was now charged with the thrill of unseen
Danger, and camaraderie of flight.
It was just a game—but being a serious
Child, the one charged with oversight
Of the exit, I ran as if scouting the perilous
Path of an army forced back dazed from the wars,
Past my classmates down the hall to the doors.

    A pageant gleamed while I held the fire
Doors open: all those laughing boys
And girls grew up, grew old; their entire
Lives passed in a stream of sorrows and joys
As they rushed on down the stairs, and were gone.
Watching them pass, I could not believe
How many marched to oblivion,
How many deaths there remained to grieve.
But then a schoolgirl cried, "It's Tuesday morning,
And we're just practicing, just practicing."

CHARLIE SHAVES HIS BEARD

One morning Charlie woke up
and to his own surprise
decided to cut his beard off.
Like an outworn disguise
it seemed best to let it drop—
ten years was quite enough.

His eyes and face grew tense
and he felt a little dizzy—
his gaze stared down the gazer
as the mirror shared with Charlie
a mute intimation of violence
from scissors and the razor.

His beard, still brown if dappled
gray, was lathered white
as a sheep set to be shorn;
he clutched the scissors tight
yet still his fingers trembled—
his mask was gouged and torn.

The razor's turn—first blood!
Scraping through the stubble
in search of the buried chin
the fresh blade hit trouble—
a red rivulet flowed
out from the startled skin.

Right side shaved, the mirror
showed him a mad hermit
bleeding in frosty muck
after a thaw, unfit
for civilized sight—his error
left him gaping dumbstruck.

But too late now! The whiskers
had to go altogether.
Spare the moustache? No,
he just slapped on more lather
and shaved it—better or worse,
the whole mask had to go.

He washed his bewildered face
as a midwife bathes an infant
fresh to the world, and stared
at this newfound confidante—
what stranger had taken his place,
grin so brazenly bared?

Time's work, done best in secret,
had left deep lines behind.
Cautiously, Charlie tried
his new mask on to find
if he could stand bare naked
and still manage to hide.

THE COUGAR

At dawn I took my boat and crossed
Over to Sonora Island. No one
Lives there now since the last logger
Left, and the young firs and pines
Hide the deer well. I held my gun
Loose as I hiked a road long lost
In moss and nettles, watchful for signs
Of deer. I never heard the cougar.

I was the only man on the island
That day in November. It felt good
To walk alone into the breeze
And drizzle, kicking away the brown
Alder leaves blown from the wood
To the path. Where a creek spanned
The road I paused, and knelt down
To drink. Something made me freeze.

Slowly, slowly, I turned. The great cat
Who followed behind was watching me.
He crouched low and long on the road,
Low and long and golden against
The leaves, watching pensively,
A damp sphinx of the woods. He sat
So still, tail sinuous, that I sensed
He could watch me forever; or explode.

Meant for the moon, those yellow eyes
Glowing through the pale light of noon,
Those eyes meant to prowl the dark
Met mine in mutual appraisal—
One man on an island paused to commune
With one cat. I spoke first. "A wise
Cat does not trifle with a loaded rifle."
He listened quietly to my remark.

But the cat did not bother to answer.
I aimed, and touched the trigger, waiting—
For what, I could not say. A man,
A cat, we shared some time alone;
I lowered my gun, reciprocating
His silent gaze. The golden panther
Moved off through the trees, and was gone.
I camped there, and listened to the quiet rain.

THE FARMER GORED BY HIS BULL

In memory of Mr. Len Carlson, who died December 22, 1965,
on his farm in Glen Valley, British Columbia

Golden one, that thrust you gave that first
Slipped through my heart caught me by surprise
And held me there, listening to the burst
Of veins feeding a warm flood on the rise.
So many changes now—your black-tipped horn
Turned red, my soul turned free, my wondering eyes
Wide open everywhere. My body, shorn
Of weight and years, is just a visitor,
Joined by a silvery thread with this newborn
Beast we have made, our coupled minotaur—
A bull's head hoists the body of a man!
I know your labyrinth, unraveler;
Below, the world lies open to my scan—
I see how all that ended first began.

So strange, that I who raised you from a calf
Have now been raised by you! You tossed me high
To lay me low—I wonder, should I laugh
To see what comes to pass, or should I cry?
We were meant for a time when danger bound
To beauty made that beauty multiply.
I saw the way those pointed glories crowned
Your head, lit up your eyes, sparked a wild beat
That set your black hooves stamping on the ground.
To cut them, burn their roots, would bring defeat
To both of us—without his horns a bull
Is half without his sex, left incomplete,
And I, I would have missed the miracle
Of seeing you so strong and beautiful.

But still, I pierced you first. I shoved that steel ring
Clean through your nostrils, clamped and locked it there,
Locked the surging strength of the tawny yearling
To human will, and made you so aware
That strength will yield to pain—yes, where I led
You followed, though your nostrils still might flare.
While I could hold you, many times instead
I let you loose to prance across the field
With horns that dazzled every cow you bred
And harried shadow rivals, made them yield
To you, my minotaur! Oh, we were friends
At play this wintry day when you unreeled
The silvery thread and showed me as it ends
Strength sometimes bends, but beauty rends, it rends!

THREE SOLILOQUIES IN THE DEATH ZONE

I. In Trouble

It's hard coming down. Hard getting up. Gas,
More gas! Hell, is the valve iced up or what?
That's better, good to breathe again. It's funny
What happens—can't let go, not once you've caught
The summit fever. First try, damn crevasse
Turned me around—two years to raise the money
And got nowhere. So, three years more, then back
Again—hauled my boots onto Northeast Ridge
And camped three days there, waiting out a storm.
Altitude sick, nearly blown off the edge—
And still I had to take another crack.
But third time's lucky! Great, I'm feeling warm
And strong, that looks like Second Step already—
Here's a good rope to clip to. Everest!
You're mine today, made me the tallest man
In all this world—I stood and shoved my fist
Up into pitch blue outer space and—steady!
Loose rock... traffic ahead—a caravan
It looks like. Have to wait while they get by.
Ten thirty now—lots of time to get down.
Hold on... rope's tangled—let me just unclip
And—falling!
                    God, where am I? Must have flown
Up here—Dad said I ought to learn to fly
And now I have. My head—stop, get a grip!
Need oxygen, need oxygen, need ox—
Canister's empty I guess, isn't it.
Slow down, slow down, just take it nice and easy.
It's fine up here. Just need to stop and sit
Awhile. Dad—did you call? Behind these rocks—
A cave—here's Mr. Green Boots. Stomach's queasy.
Mind if I join you? Thanks, I'll rest awhile.
You made it too? That's great. A nice breeze here.

17

It's warming up, let me unzip my coat,
Take off these gloves, who needs this useless gear....
Look at them all, climbing up single file—
Hi Dad—can we go sailing on your boat?
Your friends are hauling up the anchor line.
Meet my pal, he's dying to sail with us.
The ocean's warm, I bet, way down below.
Maybe a swim—let's climb aboard, cast loose
And take a cruise. We'll have a blast, so fine
To... Dad? Wait—where did everybody go?

II. Summiting

Over Third Step, and there's the route—it's just
A hike from here across this last snowfield—
The final victory lap! Our team is tight,
The Sherpas know their stuff—Lopsang rappelled
Four times down Second Step, then back, I'd trust
Him anywhere, and now we've got the right
Supplies up here, plenty of oxygen.
This mountain is no place for amateurs.
Nearly one—it's getting a little late.
Rick made it pretty clear that he prefers
We turn around and head back down again
By one. Won't be much time to celebrate
Up top. Kind of a shame—you plan so well
And then get thrown when someone else screws up.
Pathetic kid—must have been climbing solo,
Or packaged with some third-rate tourist group.
All out of oxygen, looked like he fell
Descending—no bones broken, tough young fellow
For sure—out of his head for lack of air,
Squatting in Green Boots Cave, his arm around
The other one like they were best of buddies.
He'd gotten half undressed before we found
Him shivering, lost—didn't have a prayer.
Nothing that we could do, but still it muddies

The climb for everyone. The fixed rope runs
Right by the cave, climbers had to unclip
To make their way on past. Forty or more,
I guess. I stopped and tried to make him zip
His vest, but he was too far gone—everyone's
At risk up here, we're climbing past death's door—
Just glance ten thousand feet down Kangshung Face!
It's hard enough to keep yourself alive,
Far less a stranger. Still, I radioed
To Rick at ABC—"Could he survive?"
I asked. Rick's been up here, he knows the place,
And what it takes to haul down such a load.
"Look, the guy's effectively dead and gone,
It's not your fault." And Rick was right.
But still it bothered me to leave him curled
Inside that cave. I think the kid just might
Have mumbled, "Dad".
                                              The snow is sloping down—
God, I'm standing right on top of the world!

III. Turned Around

Dear Cathy,
                          Coming down is easier
Knowing I'll see you soon, and though I'm writing
This in my head, back down at ABC
Tomorrow I can email some exciting
Stories before they all begin to blur.
You're wondering how it went above Camp 3,
And well, I guess I'd have to say we failed—
Got turned around a bit below First Step.
But what a day—let me try to remember....
Cathy, the stars, the stars! They seemed to wrap
The world with icy gems, so close I held
A handful in my palm. The moon brushed amber
Light along Northeast Ridge, but still we turned
Our headlamps on—by night, the fragile cornice

Of snow can lure you over Kangshung Face,
Or you might trip on lost crampons and corpses.
It's not something we talk about, I've learned,
But frozen bodies find their resting place
On Everest—too hard to bring them down—
A few end up as markers on the routes.
Ten years ago an Indian climber died
Inside a cave, and now it's called "Green Boots".
Cathy, today Green Boots was not alone!
A man, sitting cross-legged there inside
The cave at dawn, looked up at us and said
"My name is Lincoln Sharp. I don't suppose
You were expecting me." No oxygen,
No mask, no hat, no gloves, his upper clothes
Unzipped, here was a man who should be dead.
His fingers, white and rigid, glowed like ten
Wax candles. Lincoln thought he'd spent the night
On board his father's sailboat! Surely others
Passed by him yesterday. Dan looked at Phil,
Andy, Jangbu and me—were we our brother's
Keeper, or is a conscience excess weight
Eight thousand meters up in icy hell?
Nods and a radio call—turned around.
The summit was clear, hardly any wind….
The highest place, just out of reach, beguiles
The best of us, but somehow in the end
You need to climb back down with what you found
Up there, and not just what you lost.

                                    Love, Myles

PORTRAIT OF JESSE VILLAREAL

First comes the sky: swirls of turquoise and blue
Roiling across the canvas east to west,
October sun flooding the coast with light.
Curious, Jesse saunters over dressed
In Laker jacket, black wool hat askew,
Sweatpants, sporting a beard as full and white
As Santa Claus. The artist shoots a glance
At Jesse, mixes tubes of paint to echo
His jacket, hits the canvas with a blob
Of regal purple. Jesse calls, "Heh, vato,
You got good hands, your stroke got confidence."
The painter smiles, brushes another daub
Of purple on, then mixes muddy gold
To match a pair of dirty Laker stripes
That look like cool suspenders. Jesse sighs,
Hoists a whiskey bottle up to his lips.
"You got good parents, anybody told
You that? I know, I see it in your eyes."
Santa Monica pier unfolds from shore
To waves, and palm trees rise to give it shade.
The brush moves on—behind the purple figure
A coiled roller coaster serpent made
Of paint takes shape. Jesse nips a bit more
Out of his private stash—booze makes him eager
To talk. "That's how it goes, always a kid
To your own mother. 'Jesse, stay away
From chicks,' she said, 'don't mess around with girls.'
'Heh, Mom, I'm not a plumber, no, some day
I'll be a carpenter.' My grandpa said,
'You girls don't wear the pants, you just wear pearls.'
At least that's what Mom said he said, he died
Years before I was born. 'Your husband beat
On you, I catch his ass and kick it far,'
That's how my grandpa was.
                              What the—who's that
You painted? Is that me? Never thought I'd
Be someone—man, just like a movie star!"

23

THE KISS

A roaring highway disconnects
The sandy beach from a bus-stop bench,
Golden youth in springtime flower
From sidewalks home to wasted men:
There ocean air, here city stench;
There sun-bronzed bodies, here old wrecks
Whose luck ran out when pain began
To soak right through each waking hour.

A tunnel burrowing underground
Connects the beach to cityside.
A vagrant sits, all vacant stare,
Waits for a bus—to where, who knows?
Their beach-day done, two lovers glide
From out the tunnel, arms wound round
Each other's waists—the girl's face glows
As her boyfriend stoops to kiss her there.

His lips seek hers—she suddenly
Breaks free, turns, runs to the homeless one
To stroke his rough gray-whiskered cheek,
To press her lips on his in a kiss.
She slips away like the setting sun—
Just gone, with no apology.
The old man weighs his glimpse of bliss
Against a pain he did not seek.

THE SHADOW BOXER

There on the open heights he stands
    in fighting stance,
Breathes deep down to his guts and glands—
His fists held high at his temples guard
His head as he jabs and kicks back hard
    in a martial dance.

His foe sucks air to the abdomen
    and blows it out
To strike at the one who blocks the sun.
They circle together, two birds of prey—
Neither can triumph nor yet give way
    in their bitter bout.

The shadow turns in a pirouette,
    aims a kick high;
Before it lands the blow is met
And knocked aside. His own left hook
In turn is parried—each blow struck
    draws swift reply.

Wide-eyed, bare-chested, soaked in sweat,
    he stalks his own kind
Daylong, and after the sun has set
He rages on in his intimate feud.
Stars fade—still he has not subdued
    his terrible mind.

TWO PAIRS OF MARY JANES

Beyond the field he hears their laughter
Tinkling like silver summer fireflies
Darting among the skipping footfalls
That press grass down and linger after
Mother and daughter's shoes surprise
The tender shoots—their laughter calls.
Behind him, other sounds arise.

A beach years past: the sea wraps ripples
Round the man's ankles as the woman
Folds her long arms and legs round him.
His tongue laps at her wine-dark nipples.
He moves inside; she cries in unison.
Now stream and scream burst in a dim
Confluence—man, woman, and ocean.

Then afterwards, a new dominion:
Woman becomes a foreign country,
Ruled by a faint tyrannical heartbeat
Stone deaf to any man's opinion.
Borders swell to extremity.
The woman, torn, bleeds on the sheet.
Her daughter cries—quizzical, free.

He turns—now girlish laughter beckons
High up an oak. Two pairs of black
Slim shoes with rounded toes and silver
Buckles hang where the foliage thickens—
The one pair smaller, both left back.
The climbers set oak leaves astir,
At play past where his eyes can track.

VALLEY SONG

Though I miss my home on the mountaintop
    What I learned there I ponder still—
How a hard rain washes the hillside down
    But the wildfires burn uphill.

CONTROLLED FLIGHT INTO TERRAIN

Dawn up above, fog set afire below
and no one else aloft to watch it all—
could be I've died, gone back to long ago
when great birds flew, when earth was virginal—
the mist dissolves the way a silken nightdress
flutters undone, my airplane's shadow races
up the wild river—oh, I pity flightless
mortals left back asleep in human places!
This one last wilderness and open sky
belong to me—the spawning salmon lead
me on a spirit flight, skimming upstream
into a Chinese landscape scene where I
see snow-brushed mountain ledges blurred by speed
then touch the overhanging pines and dream....

REUNION

That dawn the solstice sun began its rise
Between the sacred pillars, kissed their feet
And spread its rays to lick their inner thighs,
Then lingered at the arch, its blaze complete.
I knew you then, a thousand years before
The two of us were born, the witch and priest—
Beyond that circle, through that fiery door,
We sought a path to realms beyond the east.

Once more, midsummer's sun ascends the sky—
The whirling years that toppled monuments
Of stone and buried gods without a trace
Have tossed us here, bewildered, wondering why
Amid a dying world's impermanence
We each can recognize the other's face.

GIRASOL

I

Maker of the tiger's eyes,
Have you any love or pity?
Watcher at the first sunrise,
Can you spare us love or pity?
The ancient longing to be whole
Returns to us in field and city
With every sunflower, girasol—
   With every girasol.

II

Welcome stranger, gyring round the sun!
All of us are held and hurled in the sling
   Of the sun, tightly bound as one.
      The comet voyaging
      Burns lonely through the night to bring
A swatch of glory down within our reach
And spread it on the sea, a silvery eel
      Aglow just off the beach—
Sky or mirror, which is real?

III

Cold eye! Is yours the cold eye cast on life,
On death? The comet stirs a strange unease,
   Disordered dreams and visions, rife
      With jangling rusted keys
      That open doors on auguries
Revealed to sages born in other ages—
Now I see the slouching sphinx will creep
      Yet closer while it gauges
When to make its final leap.

IV

Back, back through the helical folds of time,
Rumors sweep from the steppes, rumors of horses
    Thundering south with the comet's climb,
        Spurred on by hostile forces.
      Messengers claim to forget their sources
And astrologers tracking the skies turn pale but dare
Not carry news to the emperor, wrapped in bed
        By his concubine's long black hair—
    None dare speak what must be said.

Send for Qu Yuan! His eyes burn white,
And gazing inward see what others miss.
    The comet held in his inner sight
        Shines on the precipice
      And past it, down the deep abyss.
The emperor roused and wrathful hears Qu Yuan
Foretell his anxious kingdom's bitter fate:
        The hour at hand is when
    The dragons flee the palace gate.

Voyager through the starry night dip down
To bless this stream where Qu Yuan's body floats—
    Reflect on those who speak and drown.
        We row the dragon boats
      To nourish seers who die scapegoats
With gifts of leaf-wrapped rice cast in the river;
We merge our flickering torches with your own
        To light those who deliver
    Truths that come already known.

V

Reach down, reach down, will you not carry me
Along your fading spiral way to find
    The sun that pulls eternally?
        Be kind, I am your kind,
    How can you leave me here behind
To breathe your scent of ice and empty space?
What hope have I below when you above
        Have turned away your face
    And lacking pity spurn my love?

VI

I will live among the sunflowers now, and call
The sunflowers family—earthbound comets,
    Formed by spiraled genes like all
        Life that the sun begets;
    And from its rise until it sets
The flowers of gold will turn to face the sun,
And they will blaze right here upon this earth—
        Bright as the comet's run—
    Auguring the next rebirth.

beautiful broken things

THE PRIVATE LOVES OF MR. AND MRS. CHEN

"Daughter, go close the blinds!" cried Mrs. Chen
One springtime morning when she began to die
In earnest. Puzzled, Dienlin asked her, "Why
Do you lie so late in bed today, and when
Will you come downstairs? Look at the world outside—
Below the mansions high on the slopes, the towers
Of commerce gleam—right now, from one of ours
Father watches his laden freighters glide
Through the harbor. Come and watch them too,
Drifting like seabirds beneath the dragon-green
Mountains that crown the peninsula."
                                        "I've seen
Those ghost ships sail—I've held the world in view
So long," sighed Mrs. Chen, "but love has fled,
So draw the blinds down tight on my death bed."

> *A springtime rain never*
> *Felt so fresh and warm*
> *As the time that young man's*
> *Voice first made me quiver,*
> *Caught me up in his storm*
> *Of dreams and bold plans.*

"She's old," the doctors said, "so old and frail."
They went away. Day after day Dienlin
Washed her, combed her hair, set her hairpin,
Carefully polished her every fingernail.
Early each morning Mr. Chen dressed up
In suit and tie, then sat in her corner chair
And watched over them. He sometimes said a prayer.
All day he watched, and only would sip a cup
Of tea that Dienlin brought him. Finally
His daughter pleaded, "Father, come speak to mother!
She grows so weak—there may not be another
Chance."

43

"Too late," he said, "she can't hear me."
Next morning at dawn, after his wife had died,
Mr. Chen still sat in her corner chair, and cried.

Two wild orchids pinned
In her long black braids
Brightened the village lane—
I grew jealous of the wind
Furtively stroking that maid's
Soft face, damp with spring rain.

FOR THE LAST SOLDIER KILLED IN A WAR
SINCE FORGOTTEN

A bullet through a soldier's brain
    keeps him safe from pain
and dust will serve as well as mud
      to cover blood.
      Let wind and rain
    wear away the stain
on foreign ground, and never let
    some lingering regret
disturb the holidays back home—
      don't exhume
      old grieving now,
that grave's forgotten anyhow.

A baffled king who spoke with God
    sent him under sod,
brought him home on a midnight plane
      to be lost again.
      His father stood
    and dropped a single clod,
listened to it echo long
    until that too was gone.
After grave and heart were closed
      he dreamed the ghost
      of his soldier son
came back to ask if the war was won.

Won or lost, it's all the same
   once no one's left to blame.
"The king is dead—long live the king!"
   the children sing.
   It's such a shame
   the dead can't join our game—
wrap Peter in a shiny flag
   to make a body bag
and lay him out beneath the hill;
   then he keeps still,
   we let him stay,
and softly, softly, steal away.

BUBBLE'S BURST

At dawn that last of days no trumpets sounded,
Or maybe they were drowned in wicked wind.
Though lookouts stared, they spied no spectral horsemen—
Perhaps some hid, well-cloaked inside infernal
Coiled clouds, but no one came. If we had sinned
We weren't told how. Newspapers all propounded
Their theories: sunspots, global warming, normal
And cyclic ice age, like before the first men.

Plain awful weather. Rain, at first a torrent,
Stopped cold as if the heavens were drained of pity.
And something strange was happening up in space—
Satellite signals died, computer networks
Crashed, and the multitudes who filled my city
Felt very lonely. Through the day the abhorrent
Cyclone toyed with the earth the way a cat works
A mouse—pouncing, clawing, licking its face.

Schools let out early, government buildings closed.
The wind grew steady, spun a tightening noose
Round the Tropic of Cancer west to east—
A fevered dervish dancing on the world,
Genie without its master broken loose,
Freed from its bottle, with blind passions roused.
The sun dimmed in green neon sky to herald
Endless dark, and up from the swirling beast

Tornadoes shot like missiles to the void.
A lone voice cried, "Oh, the bubble's burst!"
And then the great wind sucked earth clean of cattle,
Children, nations, poems, oceans and air,
Lovers and prayers, the creatures of deep forest
And of the sea—sanctuaries destroyed,
Monuments broken, beaten earth stripped bare
Of soft looks and the armaments of battle.

Wandering souls still hear that cruel wind blow,
Wailing from light-years off, eons ago.

PYRAMID OF THE SUN

My steps advance
within a trance
for I am the one you bid
to mount your pyramid;
those that watch are overawed
before the feathered-serpent god
that walks arrayed in the iridescent sheen
of jade and quetzal feathers blazing green—
let me rest
before my test.

These steps ascend
to the sun's end
where I who suffered capture
am taken up in rapture,
where you that became mankind's creator
have made me your impersonator,
where the heart in my chest beats with the wild elation
of hearts that surged before the world's creation—
let me rest
my heaving breast.

Caught unawares
to mount these stairs
I who woman begot
became Quetzelcoatl:
I am the one that viewed the void
when the world was last destroyed,
I am the one that carved the holy heart
from each god so the sun's wheel would start—
let me rest
amid my quest.

I will not falter
before the altar
where at the pyramid's top
you reap a bloody crop
that ages past in flesh was sowed
to repay the debt all mortals owed
to you that soaked dry ancient bones with life
drawn out your open veins by your own knife—
let me rest
here at the crest.

Where earth meets sky
I come to die,
my four limbs pinned
in the roaring wind
as the lightning glint
of burnished flint
sends red rain rising,
crystalizing
in a crimson sun
that joins the one
of Quetzelcoatl:
two red suns blot
my failing vision
as in submission
this emptied shell
falls pell-mell—
let me rest
a mortal blest.

CRAZY NAKED WOMAN

Why were you born in this foreign country?
With roots wedged deep in the clefts of northern rock
you hold against the unsettling rains,
suck life through your chains,
and yet your limbs soar free
with the hawk.

Do you know why they call you crazy?
The north belongs to the fir and sorrowful cedar,
needles dripping and bark hard gray—
your red dress is gay
and emerald leaves shine wantonly
as they flutter.

First you flaunt your rich red raiment,
arbutus tree, then strip it off, almost
innocent in your pale green skin,
eternal virgin
who wandered by some accident
to this coast.

On summer nights the moon is an omen
low in the south between the aching curves
of your bent limbs, throwing your shadow
on waves below—
you shiver, looking woebegone
from worn nerves.

Born lost, you crazy naked woman,
meant to be swaying under some southern sky,
not to be caught in this damp forest,
far northwest—
if you could just break free to run,
and not cry!

THE HAPPY   TROUT

THE HAPPY TROUT

The trout had much to celebrate—
Not just the lure with its tasty bait
But the way the restless ripples shone
With pearls cast down by the sun at dawn.
The line stayed slack, so the fish swam free
To plunge and leap in ecstasy,
Thrilled by the gift of life renewed.
The angler's joy, though more subdued,
Revealed what the trout had overlooked:
That fish was well and truly hooked.

IN VAIN HE MOCKS THE FINE SPRING DAY

An early spring can be a bitter season.
Another hot short year is torn from earth,
Another piece of rhyme breaks loose from reason—
Neither one I count a thing of worth.
This laurel tree, all gnarled and stripped of bark,
Has now seen fifty springs; and so have I.
The tree tries on its fine green leaves to mark
The year's rebirth—I sit beneath and cry.

The daffodils are always first to flaunt
Their moist and slender stems, their golden faces;
"Withered old crones within the month," I taunt—
"The scythe will hack your last pathetic traces."
The bees are nuzzling flowers to gather pollen;
"You work and die, my friends, so why be gay?"
I wonder, though, has my own joy been stolen,
Or did I somehow give it all away?

The honest blast of winter does not chill
The heart as does this breeze that masquerades
As warm caress—I've surely had my fill
Of springtime sun, and long for when it fades.
But even now the pale bare-breasted moon
Is laughing at me through the harsh daylight:
"Don't hurry sundown, dusk will come too soon—
This spring the day is kinder than the night."

ALONE AND FREE

To be born is the earliest death.
The mother and child connection
breaks as we first draw breath—
pure union ends in ejection
 from the warm dark womb
 to a blinding tomb.

In one life we lead many lives,
and as many times we die.
Whenever the end arrives
we go out with a lingering cry
 to mourn the cost—
 that self now lost.

So it has ever been
since Adam and Eve in the garden,
though fused in love serene,
found how two hearts can harden
 from out of one
 love come undone.

The bonds we form are supple
as destinies interweave;
yet however close we couple
life will finally leave
 both you and me
 alone and free.

THE TAR PIT

These are the dark days come to grind you down.
You took a bullet—drilled clear through the heart,
Shot from behind. The wound drained out your natural
Delight and all your tears, soaking the dirt;
And still you stagger, numb and all alone.
Lost in an alley, bandits lurk and feral
Starved dogs. Now night and day the nightmares run
Together: bombed-out tunnel, exit gate
Locked tight; your home in flames, the firemen lost.
Look there! Caught in the tar, your soft black cat
Cries out as vultures bare its skeleton,
Your own feet stuck just when it matters most.

Now listen! Will you let me call you friend?
We never met and never will. But others
Have surely passed this way; though strangers all,
We've shared that grief of yours, a pain that gathers
In gut and heart as if to never end.
So listen, friend, to those who've passed through hell:
One morning, as first blur of dawn creeps in,
Breathe deep, and ask, "Now, am I lying dead?"
And if the answer comes back, "No!" that shows
You're still alive, so get up off your bed.
Walk out to meet the sunrise once again;
Go find a garden—dare to touch a rose.

MOSES BY THE RIVER

Mother, oh my mother!
Where have they gone, all those infants
set adrift in their hand-sealed baskets
to float down this unsleeping river,
    lost? One after another
they passed on by without a chance
to land, or any hope of ever
sailing back up this flood of regrets.

Mother, oh my mother!
What of me now, the fortunate one
whose basket was caught, here in the reeds?
Plucked out of the stream, I came ashore
    alone, no sister or brother.
Then strangers raised me, a foster son—
still I am a foreigner
sojourning as my youth recedes.

Mother, oh my mother!
This summer night by the river's edge
the stars spill down from the swollen sky,
they sketch your beckoning smile on the deep.
    Your arms will open to gather
me in as I wade out through the sedge—
now sing to me, sing to me, sing me asleep
with a half-remembered lullaby.

LAST RAIN

A month of steady rain
Beat on the windowpane.
The world outside stayed gray;
The year was washed away.

"It's time," my mother said.
She could not rise from bed.
My sister shot me a glance
And called for the ambulance.

Face to the sky, they bore
Her stretcher out the door,
Slowly down like a bier
Into the wan new year.

Raindrops flooded furrows
Carved by time and sorrows;
We lingered, just awhile.
Rivulets traced a smile.

FARM ACCIDENT

I. The Boy

I jump down off the step of the school bus—
      sweet stench of silage—
    and into the springtime sun.

Birds sing, a calf lows in the barn.
      The tractors are silent,
    though silo-filling's begun.

Dad's standing out on the porch with Mom—
      why has he stopped
    so early, with work to be done?

I walk on up the gravel driveway,
      slowly. Mom waves—
    what is it? I start to run.

II. The Aftermath

The kettle whistled. Violet faced the stove,
Didn't hear the door swing open and Jim
Come in. He stopped, hesitating to move,
Stood waiting for his wife to look at him.
Lifting the teapot, Violet saw him there,
Started to speak then paused, like someone up
High on a ledge, staring through empty air.
"Tea?" she asked. He nodded. She poured a cup
For him, one for herself. They sat across
The kitchen table, waiting. Violet spoke.
"They've gone?"
               "Just now." And just like that the loss
Dropped down between them; anger rose like smoke.

"What did they do, just toss him in a sack?"
"No," Jim countered, "No, they covered the stretcher,
Carried it gently, laid him in the back
Inside the ambulance." He leaned to reach her,
But Violet pulled away.

                              "You make it sound
So antiseptic—well, I saw him too,
Lying there on the concrete where you found
Him broken in a pool of hellish brew.
I'd never seen that shade before, the kind
Of sickly yellow made by mixing greenish
Silage juice with blood. It runs in my mind—
A horror movie ends but just won't finish—
The film rewinds and plays itself again."

"I wish you hadn't come," Jim said.

                                        "I had
To see," said Violet, "After all, I've been
A nurse, and how was I to know how bad
It was when you called out that Harry fell?
I thought that I could help him."

                                    "Help him? No,
Too late for that—but I just couldn't tell
You straightaway, " said Jim, "for even though
I knew the worst, the words just wouldn't come."

Something— maybe seeing her husband's shoulders
Sag as he spoke, his eyes a little numb,
Made Violet wrap his hands around to hold hers.

"But why did Harry need to work for us?
A man that age—near seventy! He'd earned
Some quiet time."

                    "He never made a fuss,
Just said he couldn't sleep unless he'd turned
The day to use. Silo-filling began,
I tried to pay him wages for his labor.
`I'm way too old to be your hired man,'

74

Was his reply, `but not to be your neighbor.'
I had to laugh, what could I say? No use
To argue! Harry's kind is nearly gone.
`Jim', he said, `your neighbor's the one whose house
Opens for you the day that yours burns down.'"

"No fire, I hope, but who'll forget that spring
Five years ago when we were flooded out—
Nowhere to go, till Harry had us bring
The whole herd to his little place. I doubt
We could have managed otherwise—a hundred
Head of Holsteins!"
                              "I know," said Jim. "His little
Place on a little hill—I've often wondered
What we'd have done with all those hungry cattle
If not for Harry. How a big flood changes
It all—I'd trade a hundred-fifty valley
Acres for twenty high ones, once the Ganges's
Over its banks! Yes, Harry, he did all he
Could to help out. It took four hours, twice
A day, to milk the cows in his old barn.
He helped alright, but gave lots of advice
I didn't need—why, every day he'd warn
Milking machines are sure to cause mastitis—
As if he'd ever used one! His own cows
Always got milked by hand."
                                        "Still, he'd invite us
Into his house—"
                        "His shack!"
                                        "Well, I suppose
That's fair, but it was home for him, and he was
Doing his best to make us welcome in it,"
Violet continued. "Harry cooked delicious
Chicken-potato soup, gone in a minute
Soon as the kids sat down. We got a place
To sleep—field for the cows, shed for the people.
We mostly needed just a warm dry space."

Violet stood up, and went to put the kettle
Back on. She saw a photo on a shelf,
Brought it over to show to Jim. Both smiled.
"Two summers back—I took that shot myself,"
Said Jim. Black and white cow, old man, a child:
The boy's arms wrapped around the Holstein's neck,
The man holding an apple with his teeth,
Tall cow stretching her tongue full length to lick
The fruit. "Yes, Harry sure was good with Keith
And all the other children too, not to mention
The cows."

        The two fell silent, let the picture
Pour out its cache of memories: the auction
Where they once bought their boy a purebred heifer,
Dawn; her summers at Harry's place where he
And Keith would teach her tricks, like rolling over,
Or taking apples from their mouths; their glee
When the sweet smell of ripened apples drove her
So wild she'd dance a bovine jig to earn
Her fruit! And later, when the calf became
A full-grown cow, she got new tricks to learn—
The threesome played like life was just a game.

Jim mused, "Harry was not a farmer—sure,
He used to keep some cows, milked them by hand;
He plowed and planted seed, spread manure,
And coaxed some sort of living off the land.
Yet couldn't really farm. He kept old crones
Long past their milking days, chickens that never
Laid a fresh egg. The fields were full of stones
And stayed that way; his brush land by the river
Never got cleared. Machines! Oh, how he hated
Them all—tractors, balers, milking machines.
The things you need to run a farm just grated
On him—'Only good for grease on your jeans!'
He'd claim. Why was it him today that climbed
Up that ladder to pitch the silage? Who'd

Want to sweat inside the silo, begrimed
And breathing dust? That was his attitude—
He'd rather pitch the grass than stand and watch
A tractor run a big new-fangled unloader—
Machines and Harry, they just didn't match!
I would have climbed myself to spread the fodder
So he could have the easy job below.
Harry—damn! He just wouldn't hear of it."

Jim held his brow as if he didn't know
What more there was to say to Violet,
To make her understand. But she, as if
To say there was no need, just brushed his arm
And gestured to the door. They caught a whiff
Of silage—odors of a working farm—
Mingled with early roses near the porch.

"There was a woman, long ago," she said.
"Things didn't work—she left him in the lurch.
Once he told me a bit. His eyes were red."

"He never spoke of it to me. But then,
Men seldom speak to men. Not that way. Still,
Some people hide their sadness with a grin.
I wonder—maybe Harry had his fill."
"What do you mean?"
                                  A train the other side
Of Fraser River passed by with a moan
That slipped through cottonwoods and crossed the wide
Gray stream—the sound of someone leaving home,
Who wasn't coming back.

                              "Oh, nothing, really.
It's just—lately, it seemed like more than age
Made his step slower. Life in our small valley
Is changing fast—it makes it hard to gauge
What's coming. Harry felt there's too much new.
Could be he just let go."

From down the way
Dust from a school bus rose. Now Violet drew
Closer and whispered, "Jim, what do we say?"

III. The Fall

One thought
stillborn
in a freefall
dream,
one thought
that's all,
no time
to scream
or say
goodbye
or wonder
why,
no last
regret,
no gift
to give
nor loss
to grieve
and yet—
and yet—
I want
to live!

the damp cellar

A BIRD HATCHES

In glory of genesis
the oval universe
took form surrounding me,
and I was born to bliss
inside the mother yolk
where bathed in tranquility
I felt my world immerse
me in soft nectar, soak
me in warm sustenance,
in nurturing abundance.

There is bread not of this world.

But as swollen cells divide,
now multiplied to make
me large, articulated
with heart and lungs inside
my skeleton and skin,
my world is dissipated
and I can only slake
my thirst with bitter poison—
these limbs that I was given
break on the dome of heaven!

There is bread not of this world.

Despairing, my beak cracks
the vaulted firmament,
my rotted paradise gives way;
claws rip it wide and clamber through to climax
in waves of air and light
that flow forever, flow by night and day
to lift the feathered ones in their ascent
to heavens reachable by flight.
Here food and drink are mine; yet still I wonder,
will these new heavens also split asunder?

There is bread not of this world.

81

WATER RIGHTS

Crossing high Nevada desert I came
To some hardscrabble town set in a waste
Where long ago a miner staked his claim.
A road to nowhere—just some trailers braced
Against the desiccating wind, gas station,
Church, post office, tyrannized by sun
Year after year. Amid that desolation
Water was almost never seen to run—
Except in one small irrigated patch
Of lawn where rows of planted willows shaded
Marble slabs, green guardians keeping watch
Above townsfolk who'd lived, and loved, then faded.
    The living thirst for water, yet instead
    Take greater comfort moistening their dead.

KINGDOM OF STONES (Utah Canyonlands)

Here lies a kingdom built when neither king
Nor slave yet lived to tread upon these lands,
Before the earth was gripped by human hands
That claimed the right to plunder everything.
Gaze through these red stone arches opening
A passageway to where that castle stands—
Hoodoos, set on the hillside it commands,
Form terracotta warriors in a ring.

Though nothing that you see—this citadel
Of stone, these feline dunes of rock aligned
Like sphinxes in a row, that sentinel
On constant guard—was made by humankind,
These stones were just the raw material,
Their meanings forged inside the human mind.

ST. GEORGE'S ROTUNDA, SOFIA

Enemies still conspire to intercept
Each other here, in ancient Balkan places,
Where gods of battle sent their hostile races
From west and east to clash and die unwept.
Yet here, through all the wars, St. George has kept
His sanctuary. On the dome, mere traces
Of faded angels bound black empty spaces
To form—a gazelle!—etched just as it leapt.

What painter drew that antelope in flight?
Did he even see the beast between
His angels—forms now almost out of sight?
Creator dead, new births take place unseen
As figure fades to ground, and gaps unite
To mold new shapes the artist did not mean.

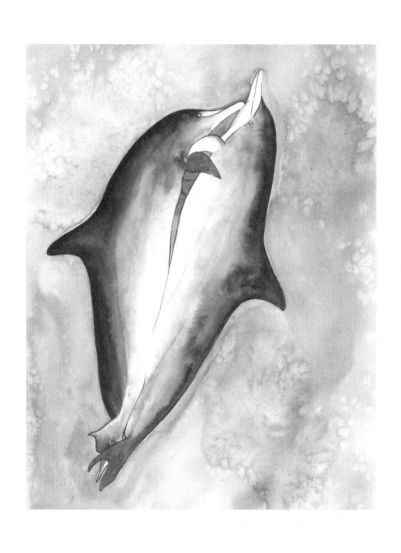

IN THE GULF STREAM

Afloat on the warm wet bed of the sea,
   soothed by fingering ripples
      flowing south,
the water shimmering over me
   laps my stiffening nipples,
      salts my mouth.
Between my legs, between my breasts,
   a sinuous motion follows—
      dolphins break
skyward through the foamy crests
   to plunge back in the hollows.
      They overtake
me in the stream, and each in turn
   with upward thrust reveals
      my hips to the sun,
then drops me down to splash and churn
   the ocean that conceals
      what has been done.

MALIBU EVENING

Above a sea cliff wrapped within the arms
Of hills I watched the final flaming plume
Of sun get quenched in waters off Point Dume.
Night fell—I saw the moon fashion strange forms
Traced from another life. A sultan's child,
His firstborn son, his dark sultana's pride,
I wandered free inside my lush seaside
Harem garden, bathed in fragrance of wild
Hibiscus blossoms. Rows of towering jinn
Wielded palm fronds as fans. Winds from the desert
Warmed me, kissed my nape, and turned into expert
Lovers' fingers stroking my hair and skin.
But then a distant sound, a serpent's hiss,
Drew my eyes to the hills: there red-haired gorgons
Raged at me, their tresses satanic organs,
Hot writhing snakes devouring paradise.
My back to the sea, standing all alone,
My heart first turned to ice, then ice turned stone.

THE WILDLIFE TREE

Faller, spare that tree
from some dead generation—
let it alone to be
the first seed of creation.
That ancient tree's been burned,
blistered, scarred and beaten,
its gnarled branches turned
into soft flesh eaten
by grubs; it's limbs are home
to owl and to woodpecker,
to bees and their honeycomb.
Its twisted trunk was thicker
than any other fir,
its green crown sat higher;
now this progenitor,
survivor of drought and fire,
stands by itself again.
One tree alone—but alive—
recalls the origin
of forest, how to revive
it after desolation.
Let all that live in groves,
in packs, or civilization
look out for their own troves
of wisdom time has scarred—
the darkening sky may redden,
so who might still stand guard
the day after Armageddon?

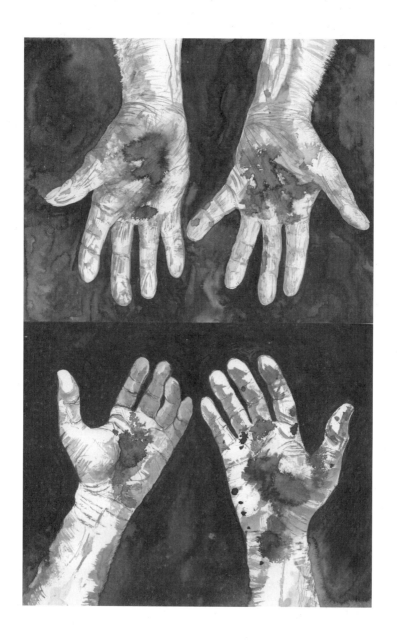

BLACKBERRY SEASON

"Tell me, old man," the young man asked,
"You who have wandered the world so long,
And through long days and nights have basked
In whatever joys you found among
    Life's sorrows, what gives pleasure
      In greatest measure?"

The maple's red, and the tall grass withering—
Do you hear the wild geese gathering?

"Follow me, son, to the marginal places
That no one bothers to plant or tend,
The roadsides, fences, dikes and ditches
Where blackberries ripen at summer's end,
    Fruit free to whoever scrambles
      To reach the brambles."

The days close in, the nights are lengthening—
Have you seen the wild geese gathering?

"But a blackberry patch is a no-man's-land,
Old fool, where the tendrils tear at your clothes,
Where the blood-red thorn leaves a bloodied hand
And the blackest berries are always those
    That hang, so ripe and tender,
      In unreachable splendor."

Fog in the morning, and the rabbit shivering—
Wild geese in the fields are gathering.

"Just so, young man, is the sweet delight
Of a purple tongue made sweeter still,
For in blackberry season it takes a fight
To taste the best—and where's the thrill
    In the end, my friend, if not for
      What's free but fought for?

A pale sun, and the deep dew glistening—
In the sky wild geese are gathering.

GRIZZLY

She-bear on a gravel bar
Rakes swollen salmon from the river,
Broken bodies left to quiver
On the stones with mouths ajar,
Their salmon-urge, the quest to spawn,
Crushed between indifferent jaws.
Sullen, the grizzly overawes—
All must wait till she moves on.

Out of nature draw a symbol—
The claw that rips right through the salmon
Carves the mind to shape an emblem
Of what we fear, and yet resemble.

HERONS

Cloud break at dusk—
a pair of herons
journeying
out of time,
beyond recurrence,
caught in their climb—
there! On the wing
through endless dusk

They rise in shadows,
rise up forever,
their incantations
binding sky
and earth together
in a synchrony—
long vibrations
of winged shadows—

As though this world,
this circling stillness,
still held to a path
cleft by great birds
out of a fullness
lost when words
took shape from breath
to cloud the world.

WOLVES' SONG

Brothers and sisters join my song,
    Sang the old gray wolf to his kin,
Treasures gleam in a wolf's fresh dung
That never before were seen—
New beauty shines when the flesh dissolves,
    Purified by wolves.

These glittering white shards of bone,
    The old wolf sang again,
More precious now the flesh has gone
Where flesh cannot be seen,
Gained luster passing through ourselves,
    Purified by wolves.

So we're your hope of redemption, friend!
    Cried the wolves in unison,
For when we meet we aim to grind
New jewels you've kept unseen—
What bares the bone the flesh absolves,
    Purified by wolves.

THE ARBUTUS AND THE FIR

This too is a kind of love:
by the sea, on a rocky shelf
an arbutus wrapped herself
around a fir tree, wove
for him a cloak of her soft
leaves to drape his foundation.
The fir ignored her passion
as his gray unbending shaft
drove upward to the sky;
yet still she clung to him
with every leaf and limb.
Long years cycled by
until the leveling wind
that seeks out those too proud,
finds those who stand unbowed
and all who scorn to bend,
blew down the cold fir tree.
His lover caught his fall;
together, roots and all,
they plunged on down to the sea.

TO THE ISLANDS

I want to sail south to the Pender Islands
On ebb tide in the autumn afternoon;
There still is daylight left, if I leave soon,
To reach Bedwell Harbour by close of day.
I want to hold the wheel in my two hands
And run the boat alone—I know the way.

I hear the fading cries of summer children
Who rode and laughed beside me on the water,
Watching the bobbing head of a sea otter
At play in gardens of deep purple kelp;
Those summer cries that will not sound again
Call me back down this stream like cries for help.

I want to smell the cedars with the sea,
To watch the sunlit waters turn so gold
That I forget how deep they are, and cold;
I want to glimpse an orca's gleaming arc
Before it plunges back in mystery
Beneath the anxious bosom of the dark.

Headed down the channels of Georgia Strait
Green islands fade to blue, to gray, to sky
And clouds where I am lost, a passerby
Between the land, the mirror, pale mirage—
Where I've forgotten how to navigate,
Forgotten where to find safe anchorage.

And there's no stopping where deep water flows—
All those who ever moved upon the ocean
Have learned that life is never-ending motion;
A boat unpowered is left to slowly drift
Against the rocks, or founder in shallows,
As fickle wind and current chance to shift.

Moonrise! A seaway strewn with precious stones
Shows me the way down south; and if I pass
The Penders in the night on seas of glass
I'll journey on to islands not yet seen,
Hear ravens calling out from bleached whale bones
To sailors landing where they've never been.

IN THE DAMP CELLAR

When shaken by a vision
they mocked me in derision;
when I let slip my dreams
they called them idle schemes—
so I keep my dreams to myself
downstairs on a cellar shelf
left damp to sprout or go rotten
but still not quite forgotten.

CLEARING THE PEAT

I

A bog-born boy crawls
Out of the peat, out from those pools
That overflow with night
From day to darkling day beneath the brutish
Underbrush, following a trail of mucus jewels
Secreted beneath the tree-falls
By a golden slug who shares his wish
To find sunlight.

Feather, fern and fairy-dust
Are dying, dying down to merge
In the mire's damp humus bed,
To meld together there beneath the fog
And beneath a sea of moss broken by the dark surge
Of mushroom and the seedling's thrust—
All gathered in those pools of tears the bog
Can never shed.

One glimmer caught, the slug
Turned back to the bog land, but not the child—
He grew in the sun's sweet joy
Until, full-grown after seasons in the sun,
He knelt by a marsh, and learned from a golden slug beguiled
By the light that this man who dug
With bare hands in the peat had begun
A bog-born boy.

II

"Son, we need more land—I figure it's time
To clear the peat. We've got to make more hay;
Even our back bog land—more slime and grime
Than soil—might work if we just find a way

To clear the brush and drain it. Wild skunk cabbage
Never has fed a cow—not poison mushroom
Neither! That wasted acreage could yield silage
After we clear it. The soil, it won't be rich loam,
Fertile and dry enough to grow alfalfa,
But I hear peat can take canary grass—
Piss-poor fodder, sure, but still a helluva
Lot better use than swamp weed pumping gas
Into a cow's belly. Won't feed the milking
Herd, I know, but good enough for the heifers,
And if it helps the haymow last till spring
We can afford the grain a cow prefers
Over corn silage."
                    "Dad...."
                                "Yes?"
                                        "Do we have to?"
"I played there too, I know, son—it's a boy's
Kingdom—I wish that we could put it off to
Next year. It's hard, but we don't have a choice."

We struggled through July, between the first
And second crop of hay—a boy, a man,
A John Deere tractor. First day out, Dad cursed—
The tractor spun its wheels and then began
To sink, down and down to its axles, resting
There, a steel green hippo basking in mud.
I hated that infernal bog for besting
My old man—his jeans got coated with crud
When he waded on in, trying to dig
The wheels out. Then I trudged for three long miles
To fetch a neighbor's tractor, hooked a big
Chain to our own. We both broke into smiles,
Our hippo freed. "A tactical retreat,"
Said Dad. We took the rest of that day off.

And so it went, all of July. The heat
Would drain our sweat out almost fast enough
To refill stagnant pools we hoped to drain
With ditches dug by hand. And it got wetter
Deeper down in the peat, although no rain
Fell all that month. Slimy water would splatter
Our clothes and drip down into our gumboots.
Dad hacked his way into the bush to chainsaw
Trees down; the tractor then pulled out their roots.
At month's end, peering down into the main maw
Of our farm's bog, Dad stopped and called a truce.
"It's time to cut second-crop hay, so let's
Circle these five cleared acres in a noose
Of fire, and burn it clear. That slug there gets
To keep some of his bog a little longer."

We spent one more day, worked to clear a firebreak
All round. We tried the plow—the peat was stronger.
It choked the plow-blade, made the old John Deere ache,
The tangled fibers hardened into sinews
Just like my father's arms. After we could
Clear a wide circle, Dad plunged through the fen ooze,
Poured gasoline to soak the fresh-cut wood.

It didn't catch when Dad dropped the first match,
But blazed at last. All week the flames danced high,
Then seemed to fade. That August I would watch
The distant smoke out back and wonder why
It lingered on. "The peat's caught fire," my father
Told me, "No telling how long peat will burn."

September came. I watched the rain clouds gather
Off in the west, and strained hard to discern
The line where smoke turned into cloud, but lost
Sight of their border. Fall rains seemed to kill
The fire. Come spring, though, smoke rose like a ghost—
Peat fire burns slow; down deep, it's burning still.

III

Sang the slug to the moon, to the moon far away,
    "We are old, we are old,
      Shining bright as we sway,
    For none is more gold, is more gold.

"These mothers and daughters, these fathers and sons,
    Sleep quiet tonight
      As we watch them and play
    In the gold of your golden moonlight."

"Where but the mire holds water and fire?
    Join us soon, join us soon,
      At the close of your day,"
    Sang the slug with the moon, with the moon.

night vision

JEST OF GENESIS

Perfect stillness. Deep in timeless
silence a spark ripped genesis
from the virgin void, peace destroyed
as the first surge of overjoyed
explosion thrust us dust into motion
out on the chaotic space-time ocean.
Carried along on waves of song
strummed on the lyre and struck on a gong
we danced to the universal choir,
danced in a gyre lower and higher
becoming stars to burn and freeze
in nebulas and galaxies,
becoming the sun and giving birth
to this rich earth, where pain and mirth
took form in flesh to endure its test.
Shaken awake by the manifest
jest of genesis, the word
of life and death, our hearts are stirred
by a whispered rumor, news that sends
sharp shivers— "All that begins, ends."
Our cognizance fails, we lack sure answers,
yet no regret besets us dancers—
of all the dust in this crazed creation
whatever danced with such wild elation?

FALLING-DOWN DRUNK

I ran with a bottle in my hand
right down the ragged center line
between the lanes of cars that fanned
night breezes, dodging the looming white
headlights that tried their best to entwine
the red taillights that screamed on past
like tracer bullets on my right—
yes, I was running strong until
that twisted highway lurched and tossed
me hard, face down in a soggy ditch.

I was alright—I stood up still
holding my whiskey bottle safe
and downed a shot to ease the itch
I felt. I leapt a barbed-wire fence
and tore my pants. But clothes just chafe
the skin—I stripped them off and ran
bare-naked through the night of dense
late summer grass and ripened fruit.

I ran to where the full moon shone
down on the laden trees of an orchard.
A woman knelt and played the flute—
the melody her red lips traced
gave such fine pleasure as she tortured
me there that I felt dazed by the tune.
We shared a drink—I got to taste
the silver apples of the moon.

LET SEPARATED LOVERS CHANT TO SHARE DREAMS

Chant, chant, enchant with me,
One dream together we will see;
Our bodies lie tonight apart
But dreams come from a single heart.

We each lie on our separate bed,
Man and woman head to head,
    Chant, chant, enchant with me,
I feel my face to be your face,
I feel these sheets as your embrace,
    One dream together we will see.

Sound asleep, our bodies curled,
We slip into the water world,
    Chant, chant, enchant with me,
Until the moon has crossed the sky
Let visions merge from eye to eye,
    One dream together we will see.

Woman lake, and man the stream,
Mingle waters as we dream,
    Chant, chant, enchant with me,
Fix the visions that we make
So we remember when we wake,
    One dream together we will see.

Chant, chant, enchant with me,
One dream together we will see;
Our bodies lie tonight apart
But dreams come from a single heart.

THE WEDDING CEREMONY

Maiden fair, the sun's delight,
Have you come to die tonight?
These shadows you are dreaming of
Slipped past the guardians of love.

The execution chamber cruel
Looms just beyond the vestibule;
The priest awaits, the bridegroom too;
He trembles at the sight of you.

You wear your alabaster gown,
Hair braided in a golden crown;
Your cashmere sweater, color of rose,
Subdues the chill that through you flows.

What is this place? What happens here?
You clasp your bridesmaid's hand in fear,
Together crawling through the door
To fall prostrate upon the floor.

The priest is pointing to a cross;
Its empty arms now speak of loss
As crumpled over in despair
It beckons to embrace you there.

The finger moves, the bridegroom knows
That power deep within him grows;
On top the altar he unwraps
The sacred tool, the silver axe.

The time has come to bid goodbye;
Your cashmere sweater, lifted high,
Becomes a present for your friend
Who shares your grieving at the end.

Your bridesmaid's Asiatic hair
Is blacker yet than yours is fair,
And for a moment hides your face
Uplifted in the last embrace.

Your lips touch hers, then pull away,
For you must go while she must stay;
Alone you draw up on your knees
To take the blow and hope to please.

He first shakes loose your golden crown
And lets your hair come tumbling down;
With eyes half-closed you draw the breath
That forms the bridge from life to death.

The stroke that opens up your skull
Lets out a pain that now feels dull;
Your wound becomes a wondrous eye
That sees beyond the earth and sky.

NIGHT COMES TO POINT DUME

Seals call from the rocks as sinuous rows
of dolphins weave their dark designs in the ocean.
The evening sky is painted red with seashells,
a blood-red tide rising to flood the sun.

Seals fall silent, the undulating motion
of dolphins fades. A night without stars flows
into the world till sea and sky are one.
Seabirds nod to sleep on slow swells.

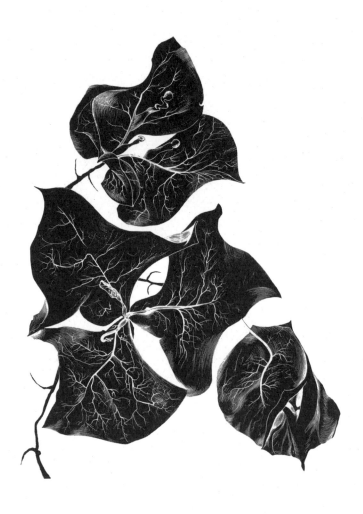

BOUGAINVILLEA

This might have been a dream:
blossoms of bougainvillea
with thorns on every stem
crowned a sunlit cupola
to form a purple diadem,
and though my palms turned raw
I grasped the vines and climbed them—
once at the top, I saw
the flowers pulsed with venom.

RUNAWAY HORSES

The first trembling passed through horse to rider
As clouds sidled across the wordless face
Of a full moon. She felt the man beside her;
His black Arabian matched the nervous pace
Of her own sweating roan, their path now lost
In damp and darkening woods. Just then a cloud
Compressed the moon; both horses neighed, and tossed
Their heads, straining to reach the crystal rod
Of light that pierced the leaves of gray birch trees.
They broke into a canter. Tree-tops moaned
With siren lips; some wild hope seemed to seize
Their bolting hearts. Their hooves slashed the soft ground,
The reins fell slack—the riders gripped the manes.
Below the woods thinned out; the dark ground sloped
Down through streaming moonlight to open plains
And then the sea. Onward the horses galloped
Towards the cliffs, and launched in a stark tableau:
Legs still pumping, their riders' arms extended
Up to the stars, mirrored in waves below,
Where equine throats burst into song, then ended.

THE DAWN OF SPACE FLIGHT

A naked boy on a sea rock,
watching the stars afloat
below his feet and above him,

saw twin hunters stalk
the great bear and his brother;
he saw white arrows shot

across the mirrored rim
of heaven pass right through
his own shadow in the water.

He watched as an aura grew
radiant around his head
as if he too had become

a spirit inhabiting
some intimate astral realm,
until at last the boy knew

he could break right through the film
that cuts earth off from heaven.
Then breathing deep, he spread

the slender wings he was given
and flew down into the stars
like a chieftain guiding the helm

of a longboat on its course
through phosphorescent night.
The boy plunged through the riven

dipper on down to the light
of the north star and beyond
to the great void that endures

where no sun ever dawned.
In that black watery place,
at the end of his headlong flight,

the first astronaut found
how cold it is in space.

TERRORIST HEART

"Tyrant! Master of denial!"
cries heart to head, "You rule
the long cold march of days,
mock me and call me a fool,
cast scorn with a knowing smile
and deny, deny me, always
deny me. I thirst for water,
you feed me ashes; I cry
for heaven, you show me hell
and call it duty."
                    "Why
so bitter? Why would you shatter
the peace in this house where we dwell
together?" asks head of heart.
Heart answers, "The days are yours,
but the hot-blooded nights are mine;
in the dark, without remorse,
I'll tear your world apart.
I'll burn this house, your fine
mansion—you'll watch it fall,
and when the beams have fed
the flames that dance above
us both, I'll scream, `I did
it all, I did it all,
I did it all for love!"

DESCENT

I. The Bank

"It goes in ninety seconds!" I heard a voice
Half shout, half whisper, turning my head to see
Who called; but all the people standing close

Were caught, like me, inside the machinery
Of the city bank, an ordinary crowd
Of clerks and customers lining up for money

From automated tellers. Crisp bills flowed,
Cash to prepare for New Year's holidays,
And no one spoke. The hands on a wall clock glowed

A minute to five. A man's eyes met my gaze
From down a corridor, one lupine glance
Before he disappeared inside the maze.

Chill from an open window seemed to pounce
On me. The clock showed thirty seconds left
Until.... Unsure, I had to take a chance.

My wife and daughter, lined up somewheres past
My view, right then were lost, too far away
To reach in time. Already I felt bereft.

I seized my son by the hand and cried, "Neil, stay
With me!" Turning, I fought my way out through
The throngs and reached a stairwell. Fearing delay,

I ran downstairs and out to the avenue.

II. The Street

My boy ran too, thinking it all a game.
He laughed as we reached the sidewalk, paused and turned.
Across the street, the bank tower looked the same

As when we'd entered—no one seemed concerned.
I felt quite foolish at my overreaction.
But through the next few moments my stomach churned.

Time seemed to stop dead cold, the real turned fiction.
Vague blue smoke oozed through the high bank windows;
Electric lights went dead, section by section,

Leaving gray twilight. And then my heart froze.
I stared along the darkened city canyon—
Buildings, shoulder to shoulder, leaned to enclose

The empty corridor; and from each one
Blue wisps drifted, and each had fallen dark,
As had the streetlights, and the forgotten sun.

I heard no explosion, saw no firework
Display, but simply sensed the sudden silence.
The boulevard might well have been a park:

Traffic had stopped—no, disappeared, the dense
Urban clutter gone, leaving the people
Mouthing their puzzled murmurs of suspense.

Neil held my hand, and cried, "Oh, what wonderful
Thing has happened?" I answered, "I'm not sure,"
Then realized I had to somehow grapple

With our situation. We crossed to the further
Side of the street, and found a row of public
Telephones all in use. I asked one caller

There if anyone might have sent a quick
Word to police, who surely would soon arrive
To take control. The man replied with a flick

Of finger to lips, as though he meant to give
Some sort of warning. Over at the bank
The scene resembled pictures I'd seen live

On television, news to make me thank
God I lived in America, not some foreign
Land far across the sea. Along the flank

Of the tower, through windows, I saw within
Dim figures dressed in black scanning the street.
Each appeared to hold an assault weapon,

And some had electronic gear complete
With headsets. Though blue haze obscured their faces
I felt their stares. I heard the man repeat

His warning, whispering, "They have devices
To listen in on phone calls." Taken aback,
My wife and daughter caught up in the crisis,

I'd hoped police knew of this brazen attack.
Remembering I had my own cell phone
With me, I dialed emergency to check

When help would come. But though at first a tone
Sounded, the line was busy, then went dead.
I wondered if these strange events were known

To police, the mayor, the President, who need
To serve and protect the honest citizenry.
I beckoned Neil, and turning the way that led

Out of the city, began to walk—not flee,
More like a Sunday stroll, but hoping to find
Some shelter against the growing adversity.

The night turned colder; I felt a gnawing wind
Sting my face as we walked. Later I carried
Neil on my shoulders, humming a tune designed

To lull him sound asleep. Some others hurried
Along the street as well, but fewer in number
As time passed; all grew more anxious and harried.

Then the street narrowed; our eyes began to blur,
Lost in an unfamiliar neighborhood
Where boarded windows and strewn garbage deter

Outsiders from passing through. I understood
The risks, yet hoped to find a place to rest.
Just then a bearded man emerged from a crude

Cardboard tent on the sidewalk, dirty and dressed
In rags. He shouted, raised an arm and waved.
I hesitated; but then I thought it best

To march on by, for though my body craved
Its sleep I also knew I had to guard
My son. A hazard missed beats a hazard braved—

I held to the prudent way; but the way was hard.

III. The Halfway House

My instincts served me well. In normal times
The city offers refuge and soft comforts;
It shelters us from drought and rain, and brims

With earth's rich bounty. Humankind diverts
Rivers, fields and forests to build the city,
Drying flood plains, watering harsh deserts,

And somehow holds in check its greatest enemy—
Fear—fear of the stranger by every other.
When things first fall apart the great calamity

Starts with dissolution of social order,
And then the city turns from home to cage,
A piercing look a mere knife thrust from murder.

Lines of hungry mouths become a rampage
Through the shops—the city devours itself.
When fear and want conspire to unleash rage,

Break free at once before the floods engulf
You and those you love! Escape while you can,
And hide yourself from the tooth of the uncaged wolf.

We fled the city before mobs overran
It and blocked the roads, and came to a house
Out in the country. Slipping inside to scan

The rooms, I found the house brand new and close
To finished. Furnished and stocked with food,
There was no sign of owners. It seemed their loss

In these changed times would be our gain, by rude
Law of possession. Oddly, the house lacked doors—
Doors, that final touch, still left to conclude

Construction and bar unwelcome visitors.
The great miracle was that my wife and girl
Were waiting there, as if unconscious force

Had drawn us all together despite the swirl
Of bitter decay and loss. I kissed Patricia,
And she hugged Neil, as I gave a joyful whirl

To baby Vanessa. But through the window I saw
A sight that cut our jubilation short:
A well-armed gang, some newly-formed militia,

Was camped outside. The members, wearing a sort
Of uniform, all black, were swarming around
The street and yard. We could not hope to thwart

So many attacking us, as they seemed bound
To do. I slowly drew the blinds to hide
As best we could, hoping not to be found

Just yet, and told the rest to stay inside.
Searching the kitchen drawers I found a knife
And tucked it in my belt to maybe provide

Protection. Through the doorway, after a brief
Respite, some men came in. Their heads were shaved.
Although they came unarmed, I told my wife

To wait in another room. I was relieved
To hear the eldest say the four were brothers,
Wandering homeless, caught by the gang and enslaved.

Before, they all had lived in their father and mother's
House, but it had burned in the first outbreak
Of violence. They wanted to join with others.

Were we to take them in, it could well make
The gang attack us all. "We're only a small
Young family," I said, "so don't mistake

Our open door for help." Just then a tall
Man dressed in black strode through the open doorway;
Somehow familiar, his red beret showed all

He was the leader everyone had to obey.
I took due note of the gun he kept in his holster,
Thankful he left it there. His hair was gray,

His name was Virgil; his manner conveyed some culture.
"A cup of tea, perhaps?" I dared to ask—
Virgil's restraint somehow seemed to bolster

My flagging courage. Laughing, he raised a flask
Of brandy. My wife brought glasses. In the kitchen
The three of us shared a drink. It was fine to bask

In lively conversation, indulging my yen
To talk about the times in a thoughtful manner.
With just a jerk of his thumb he sent the four men

Slinking out the door—none dared to demur;
And then he told me I must join with him,
Bring my family and be his follower.

I said, "My wife and I need a little time
To think it over." At that, though Virgil replied
With a nod, his eyes narrowed and smile turned grim.

"You have till morning, but then you must decide
To follow or leave—this house is my headquarters."
He went his way; Patricia came to my side.

"Do we stay," I asked, "and take this strongman's orders,
Or go?" She paused, then said, "You make the choice."
I thought awhile, for such a decision alters

The future in many different ways, sets loose
Consequences that cannot be undone.
"We leave at dawn," I said in a steady voice.

We sat by the window and watched the setting sun.

IV. The Refugee Camp

There's much I don't remember. January
Was mild—it snowed a time or two, I think,
But no real blizzards. Nights were often starry;

I'd wander from the campfires, stare and blink
At galaxies across the dark vastness
Of time and space. The night sky seemed to shrink

The changes we endured. I must confess
I clung to hope the changes would be reversed,
The army would come, clean up the sordid mess.

But no one came. We had to slake our thirst
For knowledge with loose rumors: maybe a coup
Had toppled the government, or at the worst,

Civilization had ended. No one knew
Anything solid; all the computers were down
And televisions stayed blank. No story rang true.

But after a shipwreck, when ocean waves maroon
You on an island, it hardly matters which rock
The ship had struck, so long as you did not drown.

Nations feel no pain, nor armies the stroke
Of the sword: each man and woman alone must bear
What comes in life. Though those we love may walk

With us some part of the way, at last we stare
At our own fate. And mine was to go to hell.
Some argue if hell is fire or ice. I swear

That hell is mud. We called it Mud Motel,
The camp where freezing rain had left us stuck
Beside the road, where thick black ooze would swell

As more refugees came. We slept in the muck.
The name was a joke—though mud there was, alright,
 "Motel" meant plastic tarps for those with luck

And bags for those without. People would fight
To escape if a passing truck was spotted.
Food was scarce; disease increased the plight

As winter dragged. The thing I especially hated
Was mud gracefully merging with shallow latrines,
The stench soaking your boots and clothes as you squatted.

Yet through the winter Patricia found some means
To keep us decent, washing clothes in the river
Upstream, using a strong solvent that cleans

Well enough, but burns the skin. And she would never
Let go of her long black hair, always washed
And combed each day. I knew how it must grieve her

To see the changes worsen. She never lashed
Out at me or the children. Money meant nothing—
Just barter or steal. I saw a man's head smashed

With a rock, blood and brains splattering
Black mud, turning it a purple color.
I pulled my knife; the killer took a swing

148

At me as well. That ended my bit of valor
But also the killer's rage; the man spat
In the mud and then backed off. I heard him holler,

"He won't eat *my* potatoes again—that's that!"
Was I to judge which man was really wronged?
The law was a rock, a knife, a baseball bat—

A gun. One afternoon, some boys had ganged
Up on another. It looked like a game of tag,
Except one hunter fired as others thronged

Around their prey, who quivering knelt to beg
The gunman to stop. When I dared intervene
The gang turned, and came after me like a plague

Of locusts. "*He's* `it' now!" one yelled, and then
The pistol was aimed at me. I ran for my life,
Through some woods and down a small ravine,

Dodging bullets as I clambered up a cliff
To the camp. Exhausted, I fell face down in the mud.
I heard my children cry, and felt my wife

Throw her body on mine; those who pursued
Me stopped and turned away. But I lay broken;
Tears poured out of my heart in a bitter flood.

Then someone laughed; I felt my shoulder shaken
By some strong hand. "Get up! You two are blocking
My fleet!" I knew that voice, and was not mistaken:

Virgil rode in a jeep; his trucks were flocking
 Behind him. "Then I told you, `Follow or leave;'
Now follow or stay." His eyes stared down, mocking—

The eyes of a wolf that had no need to deceive
His prey. I hesitated. "Patricia," I said,
"This time you choose." My wife was not naive,

Nor I—like a deer, I froze between dread and dread.
His boots were clean, and his crisp black uniform.
And then I recalled that man first glimpsed as I fled

The bank with Neil, my wife left behind in the storm;
How she and Vanessa had made their way somehow
To Virgil's house. Her eyes met his—a swarm

Of demons devoured my guts. "Get in now!"
He ordered. The children and I got in the back
Of the jeep while Virgil opened a door to allow

Patricia to take the seat beside him. The brake
Was released, the engine surged. "I am your guide,"
Said Virgil; "This is the road you need to take."

I watched the twilight glowing red, and cried.

150

Notes on Poems

The Cougar (p. 9)

This poem is based quite closely on an experience of my friend Nick Robinson, who had the opportunity to commune with a cougar on Sonora Island, off the coast of British Columbia, on November 13, 1999.

Three Soliloquies in the Death Zone (p.17)

This poem is a work of fiction, telling the story of a climbing incident on Mt. Everest from the viewpoints of three climbers. The character "Lincoln Sharp" (who speaks Part I and is described in Parts II and III) is loosely based on an amalgam of David Sharp, who died in a cave near the Everest summit in mid-May of 2006, and Lincoln Hall, who was rescued from a nearby location two weeks later. The David Sharp incident, in which a climber was left to die by many others who passed him by on their way to the summit (and back down) was by no means the first case of this sort. It did, however, become a focus of ethical controversy (drawing harsh criticism from Sir Edmund Hillary, the first person to reach the Mt. Everest summit and return alive). The striking similarity of the Lincoln Hall incident, which had a very different outcome, cast into sharp relief the moral dilemmas that arise in extreme conditions. Before rushing to cast stones at those who left David Sharp to die, due allowance needs to be made for the extreme physical difficulty of executing a high-altitude rescue, as well as for the fact that human brain function (and hence judgment) is impaired by the atmospheric conditions.

I am not a climber, but was a tourist at the base camp on the Tibetan side of the mountain in August 2006. In writing this poem I drew material from websites run by the mountaineering community, which provided such details as the origin of the nickname "Green Boots". I also was aided by John Krakauer's book *Into Thin Air*, an account of the Everest climbing disaster of 1996. (More climbers died on the mountain in 1996 than in any previous year; 2006 later claimed runner-up status in this unhappy contest.) The climbing route described in the poem, along the Northeast Ridge, is the usual approach from Tibet. On each side of the narrow ridge there is a sheer cliff (Kangshung Face and North Face). There are three "steps" on the Northeast Ridge that require climbing with hands, of which Second Step is the most technically challenging. Fixed ropes, to which climbers can attach themselves, are placed each season at technically-difficult sections of the route. The Mt. Everest summit is 8848 meters above sea level (29028 feet). David Sharp died in a cave below First Step, about 8400 meters. Lincoln Hall was rescued from a location about 200 vertical meters higher, just below Second Step.

In the "death zone", considered to begin at 8000 meters (about 26000 feet), the low air pressure and lack of oxygen make it impossible for a human to survive more than a very limited time. Because of the cold temperatures at night, as well as high winds, an overnight stay is almost certainly fatal, although a very few climbers (including Lincoln Hall) have managed to survive a night near the summit. The Sherpas are native Nepalese who work as guides for climbing expeditions; most of these are now commercial operations that charge clients large sums of money to be guided to the summit by professional western climbers and Sherpas. "ABC" is Advanced Base Camp, which on the Tibetan side is located at East Rongbuk Glacier. Camp 3 is the high camp from which a summit attempt is launched. The final assault normally begins before midnight, and hence involves night climbing.

Lincoln Hall was found and rescued on May 26, 2006, by a climbing team led by Dan Mazur, which included Andrew Brash, Jangbu Sherpa, and Myles Osborne (who two days later wrote a dispatch from ABC that provided very helpful source material).

Portrait of Jesse Villareal (p. 23)
This poem was written as part of an art/poetry project with painters Alex Schaefer and Airom Bleicher, who collaborated on a *plein air* painting done at the Palisades Park in Santa

Monica, California, in October 2006.

Controlled Flight Into Terrain (p. 33)

The title is a technical term in aviation, referring to a plane crash occurring mid-flight, not involving any mechanical failure. This poem was inspired by the crash of a small plane in the mountains of British Columbia in 2006. Ian Hollands. a pilot for an airline operating in that area, gave me some sense of how such accidents can occur. I venture to claim that this poem is the first formal sonnet to end mid-sentence.

Girasol (p. 37)

"Girasol" (pronounced "heer'-ah-sole") is Spanish for "sunflower", and in the Latin root shared with English means literally "turn to the sun." The English "gyre" was perhaps the most central symbol in the poetry of W. B. Yeats. The spiral form symbolizes cycles of birth, death and resurrection. This poem was intended as a kind of homage to Yeats at the turn of the millennium he famously anticipated in his poem "The Second Coming". I was loosely imagining the comet Hale-Bopp as I viewed it from Salt Spring Island in 1997. The spiral metric form is adapted from "Fern Hill" by Dylan Thomas. I added a rhyme scheme, *ababbcdcd*.

Qu Yuan was a poet and advisor to the king of Chu in the Warring States Period of Chinese history (approximately 300 BCE). When his attempts to stop official corruption were ignored, he threw himself into a river and drowned in protest. His frankness and devotion to duty are honored in China by a dragon-boat festival held each year in May.

Yeats was repelled by modern science, especially biology. As he died before the discovery of DNA, he never knew that the shape of the genetic code for life is a variant of the gyre—the double helix ("spiraled genes"). I found it ironic that his mystical symbol turns out to be so deeply embedded in biology.

The Private Loves of Mr. and Mrs. Chen (p. 43)

The view from Mrs. Chen's window looks down from a

house high on Hong Kong Island to the city below, and beyond across Victoria Harbour to the hills of the Kowloon peninsula. In Cantonese "Kowloon" means "nine dragons", so named because an emperor thought the hills resembled dragons.

Pyramid of the Sun (p. 55)

The massive Pyramid of the Sun is the centerpiece of the pre-Aztec metropolis of Teotihuacan, which flourished around 500 CE. It was the site of ritual heart sacrifices. Quetzelcoatl (roughly pronounced "kettzle-kwat"), one of the primary gods of the Aztecs, is believed to have had a precursor among the people of Teotihuacan. Quetzelcoatl had the form of a feathered serpent ("quetzel" is a type of bird with brilliant green plumage; "coatl" means "serpent").

A fundamental idea in Aztec religion is that the gods sacrificed themselves to benefit humankind. In their mythology, the world has been created and destroyed several times. The creation of the present age (known as the "fifth sun") began when Quetzelcoatl retrieved the bones of the dead people of the prior age and gave them renewed life by shedding his own blood on them. Our sun was created from a god who burned himself alive on a huge pyre. The sun refused to move until the other gods made a heart sacrifice. Quetzelcoatl cut open the chests of the other gods and removed their hearts, an act that set the sun in motion.

The Aztec gods required repayment for their sacrifices at the time of creation—human sacrifices. The victim, often taken captive in war, was prepared by being treated as the embodiment of a god, a "deity impersonator". This honored victim would mount the steps of the pyramid with dignity and pride. There are several landings on the way up the pyramid, where perhaps he paused. At the top, he would be stretched out on the sacrificial stone. The "fire priest" would slash open the victim's chest, seize his heart, and raise it up in dedication to the sun. The victim might remain alive a moment. His body was then sent rolling down the steps. He had become "one who had died for the gods."

156

Crazy Naked Woman (p. 59)

The arbutus tree (sometimes called the madrone in the United States) grows in the coastal areas of the Pacific Northwest, reaching as far north as the islands off the coast of southern British Columbia. I had heard that the word for the arbutus in one of the indigenous languages of the region meant "crazy naked woman". The tree has a Mediterranean look, with broad evergreen leaves, curved limbs, and red bark that peels to green.

Farm Accident (p. 73)

"Harry" is a loose amalgam of two bachelors, Harry Wright and John Snyder, both of whom lived on farms near ours in Glen Valley, where I grew up. Harry Wright died after a fall on our farm, sometime in the late 1950s.

St. George's Rotunda, Sofia (p. 87)

The Rotunda of St. George in Sofia, Bulgaria, is an ancient Christian church that dates from about 400 CE. The frescoes on the ceiling of the dome have deteriorated over the centuries. When I visited the church in 1998 I was struck by the sight of what looked like a black gazelle on the ceiling, done in the bold primitive style of a Paleolithic cave painting. The form actually consisted of black empty space between paintings of angels. As the angels in the foreground had faded away, the "gazelle" had grown out of the background.

The Wildlife Tree (p. 93)

When a forest is logged, a good forestry practice is to spare a few old trees, often from a previous growth. These trees are likely to be large but imperfect, perhaps partially rotted, characteristics that make them good homes for birds and other wildlife. Such a "wildlife tree" helps to regenerate the forest after new trees have been planted.

To the Islands (p. 105)

The two Pender Islands (North and South) lie south of Salt Spring Island. These islands are all part of a long chain in the waters of the Georgia Strait, which runs between Vancouver Island and the mainland of British Columbia. Bedwell Harbour is a safe anchorage on South Pender Island. Yet further south lie the San Juan Islands of Puget Sound, Washington State.

Clearing the Peat (p. 111)
Part III, the slug's song to the moon, was inspired by an early poem by W. B. Yeats, "The Faery Song", written in 1891.

Runaway Horses (p. 131)
The title is taken from the English translation of a Japanese novel published in 1969 by Yukio Mishima. The imagery is loosely based on the concluding section of a prose story called "The Curse of the Fires and the Shadows", from the collection *The Secret Rose* (1897) by W. B. Yeats.

Descent (p. 139)
This poem, completed on January 9, 2000, began with a dream I had in the early morning of November 8, 1999, which I wrote down almost immediately as this (unedited) note:

I was in a large bank with my family. I was with Neil; Pat and Vanessa were somewhere else. I heard a man say, "It goes in 90 seconds." I looked at a large clock on the wall. The second hand was down, it was coming up on an even hour. I thought a bomb was going to go off. I grabbed Neil and we ran down the stairwell to get out. I had no time to look for the others.

We got out. A few seconds later puffs of blue smoke came from windows, and the power went out. But it was not a real explosion. Mysterious people looked out from the bank windows. Down the street (like Wall Street) other banks had the same thing happen, all at once.

I crossed the street and found a row of pay telephones. Some people were using them. I asked someone if they had called 911. They warned me to be quiet, as the people in the bank windows were watching us. I wondered if someone was calling the police on a cell phone. Others seemed to have tried, but couldn't get through, or were brushed off. No police came.

It was dark. We went down the street, looking for someplace safe. I wondered where the rest of the family was. I saw a homeless man coming out of a hole in the side of a building. I wondered if we could hide there too, but it looked scary and dirty.

I got out of the city and went into a house. Pat and Vanessa were already there. The house was nearing completion, large, clean, and well-furnished. But it had no door. We were worried the owners would come, or people would invade it. Through the windows people were milling around outside. I tried to draw the blinds slowly, hoping they wouldn't notice us inside. There seemed to be a gang or militia in an odd uniform with a funny headdress.

Four brothers came in the entry way. They wore black, and had close-shaven heads. They wanted to stay. They said they were slaves of the gang. I was afraid the gang would come in. Their leader came in. I accosted him and tried to keep him and the gang out. They weren't very aggressive, and stayed outside.

We were all in a refugee camp. It was crowded and dirty. There was no authority. Money had no value. People were stealing. A strong man fought another and crushed his skull. I should have tried to stop him but didn't. Afterwards I reproved him. He was defiant but moved along. Some people had guns. A boy had a gun and tried to shoot me, just for fun. I ran and dodged, finally escaping by sliding down a slope through a woods. I told Pat we had to leave.

I wondered why the army didn't come. Some people thought it was a coup, and the mysterious people now controlled the army. But no one in authority came, and anarchy prevailed.

Both the content and form of the poem (terza rima) were influenced by Robert Pinsky's translation of Dante's *Inferno*, coupled with the pervasive millennial angst of New Year's Eve, 1999 (amplified by more personal concerns).

About the Author and Artist

Keith Holyoak, poet, translator of classical Chinese poetry, and cognitive scientist, was raised on a dairy farm in British Columbia, Canada. His scientific work focuses on the nature of human thinking and its basis in the brain. He has been a recipient of a Guggenheim Fellowship, and is a Fellow of the American Association for the Advancement of Science. Currently he is a Distinguished Professor of Psychology at the University of California, Los Angeles.

Keith's son Jim, who also grew up in British Columbia, is an artist trained at the University of Victoria and as an apprentice to Chinese landscape master Shen Ling Xiang in Yangshuo, China. Jim is currently based in Montreal, where he is pursuing an MFA degree at Concordia University. He has exhibited his work in Los Angeles, New York, Montreal and Vancouver, and is represented by the Glass Garage Gallery in West Hollywood. Both Keith and Jim spend part of their time at Pterodactyl Studio on Salt Spring Island, British Columbia.

Also by Keith Holyoak:

Translations from the Chinese (bilingual edition):
Facing the Moon: Poems of Li Bai and Du Fu
(Oyster River Press, 2007)

Poetry CDs from Broken Electric Records
(www.BrokenElectric.com):
Keith Holyoak's Descent (2006)
Poems of Li Bai (2007)
Poems of Du Fu (2009)

Books by Dos Madres Press

Michael Autrey - From The Genre Of Silence
Paul Bray - Things Past and Things to Come
Paul Bray - Terrible Woods
Jon Curley - New Shadows
Deborah Diemont - The Wanderer
Joseph Donahue - The Copper Scroll
Annie Finch - Home Birth
Norman Finkelstein - An Assembly
Gerry Grubbs - Still Life
Richard Hague - Burst, Poems Quickly
Pauletta Hansel - First Person
Michael Heller - A Look at the Door with the Hinges Off
Michael Heller - Earth and Cave
Michael Henson - The Tao of Longing
Eric Hoffman - Life At Braintree
James Hogan - Rue St. Jaques
Keith Holyoak - My Minotaur
Burt Kimmelman - There Are Words
Richard Luftig - Off The Map
J. Morris - The Musician, Approaching Sleep
Robert Murphy - Not For You Alone
Robert Murphy - Life in the Ordovician
Peter O'Leary - A Mystical Theology of the Limbic Fissure
David A. Petreman - Luz de Vela en Quintero
David A. Petreman - Candlelight in Quintero
David Schloss - Behind the Eyes
William Schickel - What A Woman
Murray Shugars - Songs My Mother Never Taught Me
Nathan Swartzendruber - Opaque Projectionist
Jean Syed - Sonnets
Henry Weinfield - The Tears of the Muses
Henry Weinfield - Without Mythologies
Tyrone Williams - Futures, Elections

www.dosmadres.com